The Black Man's Intervention

Volume 1

By: Aaron Fields

ISBN: 978-1-953962-12-6

CONTENTS

<u>Something To Think About Before You Read</u>

"The Black Man will always remain at the bottom of the totem pole in society until he finds his connection with God, stops seeking validation from others, creates a healthy culture in his community, and presides over his household."

----------Aaron Fields

A Word From The Author

Greetings to you, Mr. Black man, I hope you are faring well and if not; I hope you are on the way to making things better. I just want to let you know that it's important that you bring order, structure, and stability into your life. Your parents need you, your wife needs you, your brothers and sisters need you, and your children need you. God desires for you to be a powerful presence in your home, take ownership of your neighborhood, and be a force of power in your spiritual journey.

Although it's clear that most black men don't get any respect in this society, many black men are not at the top of the hierarchy. Most of them don't respect themselves or their community. Furthermore, a lot of black men keep falling for the same tricks and finding themselves in the same predicaments. Unfortunately, many African American males are experiencing difficulties managing their temper, navigating the legal system, maintaining healthy relationships, regulating their emotions, acknowledging their self-worth, and loving themselves. Drugs, alcohol, suicide, idolizing women, disrespecting women, feelings of inadequacy, and having kids without being able to provide for them all add to the decline of black men. Frankly speaking, the black man faces challenges in having faith and self-trust.

From these issues, it is apparent that many black men are facing something both internal and spiritual. It's clear that many black men are unaware of what it means to be a man. It is incumbent on us as black men to bring about a transformation. As an alternative, we have to stop placing the blame on this society and these other demographics. Above all else, we must not place the responsibility for our failings on women (black women). Even though some of them may contribute to our downfall, we still need to take responsibility and better ourselves.

As it pertains to black men, we lack knowledge of our identity, our cultural norms, and our relationship with God. Believe it or not, knowing these things will give you strength and propel you toward a prosperous future. When you lack a sense of self, the world will not respect you. Therefore, you cannot control your house, and your community looks down upon you.

You should take yourself and your life more seriously rather than relying on immature behavior. As a black man, it is your job to live a life full of purpose and to make the most of your gifts and talents. Always remember that the most valuable gift you can provide yourself and the world is to locate your purpose. As you carry on reading this book, keep in mind that we all make mistakes and none of us are perfect. We have all gone through unique experiences that shaped our lives. We should use our hardships and shortcomings to help us progress.

You've Been Lied To

Be aware that this society already expects you to fail, therefore, you will come into life with obstacles and challenges as a black man. I believe that all of you guys are gifted and talented in your own way. Be wary of others because if you're not, they will exploit your talents for their own gain. Why is that? It's because this world you live in is a lie. To put it bluntly, black men have been told lies by everyone, including himself, and even by family members. Your birth placed you in an unfavorable position due to the detrimental environment, erroneous knowledge, and obligatory beliefs that were imposed on you.

Many black men are allowing different demographics to teach them and their children about their history. As a result, these black boys go into these poor school systems that are run by people that don't care about them. Understand that these school systems ensure the failure of black boys. They don't want the black boy to perform to the highest standards because they know how gifted he is. The school system will use any means necessary to quell the creative spirit of black boys. However, they're only doing this because the black man allows this to happen. Therefore, the onus is on the black man, not the system.

Don't let the media, society, or people in your community dictate that you should be a football player, basketball player, rapper, or thug. Don't think that trying to go pro, platinum, or dealing drugs is the only way to leave the hood. There's no harm in diverging from the norm, especially if you have options. Unfortunately, society allows this narrative to exist because of the black man's permission..

Many black men were taught from a young age to fight and argue with women (black women). A lot of black men learn to accept an unhealthy relationship with a woman as the norm, but I'm here to tell you it's not natural, and it's not healthy. Many black men are taught to tolerate unacceptable behavior from the women in their lives. Gentlemen, never normalize toxic behavior from a woman because it's important that you maintain your peace of mind. If you are not in a life-threatening situation, steer clear of engaging in combat with the female, or else you could be the face of domestic violence if you make the wrong choice. To prevent all of this from happening, just stay away from the woman and concentrate on making your own life better.

Are you noticing the pattern? Most of the issues in our community result from black men not standing up for themselves and taking action. Part of the difficulty is that a good number of black men suffer from low self-esteem and will adopt a more feminine demeanor because of the single mother, matriarchal structure, as well as the lack of good male role models in the community.

Why am I saying all of this? It's because once again, black man, you have been deceived. You are made to believe that conforming to the accepted norms and obeying will lead to your care and protection by society. How is that going for you so far? Your deep-seated feeling that the world does not care about you explains why many of you black men are angry, downcast, perplexed, and let down. It's important that you concentrate on yourself and not ask for validation from this society, as you won't ever get the love and respect. Seek spiritual enlightenment rather than worldly desires. What is the point of looking for approval from a society that has no interest in you?

Bearing all that in mind, I understand you are in a difficult situation since the normal advice won't get you the outcome you desire. In order to find your answers, create your own solutions and stop depending on others to find it for you. It would be beneficial for you to find yourself in the company of other intelligent and talented black men with the purpose of helping you grow as an individual. I'd recommend exploring ways to monetize your gifts and build a solid foundation for your life. As it pertains to ownership, there is nothing wrong with a black man taking pride in something that he owns. You should not let the economic system of society restrict you. Break free and come up with one of your own. If you guys put more focus on improving your intelligence, confidence, ability to care for others, and spiritual energy, you'll be viewed as a force to be reckoned with. If you tap into your highest potential, maintain a strong connection with God, and take your place as the leader of your home and your community, then you will be unstoppable. It's the black man's responsibility to be in pursuit of truth, knowledge, wisdom, and understanding.

Do You Have A Proper Culture?

On average, what does the black man's environment look like? What elements make up his environment? Does he live in an unhealthy atmosphere? Is it destructive? Is it dysfunctional? Whatever it may be, the environment that the black man lives in is a true manifestation of how he views himself. Believe it or not, you can tell most black men hate themselves based on the way they live. Unfortunately, many black men don't take care of their neighborhoods and communities. Your spirit and the way you view yourself is going to reflect how your environment looks and how you treat others. When you see black people rioting, what's the first place they go to? They purposely terrorize their own communities. Why is that? It's because the black man has a low self image. Do you observe individuals from wealthy areas damaging their own communities? No, because they want to ensure the safety of their communities and sustain the value of the property.

Part of developing a sustainable culture is about knowing what you want. A lot of black men don't know what they truly want, but somehow they find themselves talking, complaining, and not being solution-oriented. The problem with some of you black men is that you always want to have circular conversations that don't lead to a solution. Do you really know how you feel?

Do you know what your goals are? Or do you just want to get emotional and not come up with a solution?

Why do many of you black men get upset with non-blacks that don't want to talk about race? Understand that non-blacks don't want to talk about race in relation to black people because they are preoccupied with preserving their own culture, which is something the black man should be doing in his own community. Why am I saying this? The black man needs to stop looking at other demographics to solve his problems. Some black men think that they can make progress just by having a discussion. Starting a conversation alone won't bring progress. Black men need to take action in order to solve their problems.

Are you sure you want to have a race conversation with different groups of people? I'm asking this of you because usually, the black man wants to start the conversation, but once he realizes how non-blacks really feel about him, he gets upset and emotional. You develop feelings of inadequacy because you determine your value based on how others see you as a black man. Stop seeking validation from others and stop trying to make the world love you.

Know Who You Are

One of the most important things to do as a black man is to know who you are. During times of success and prosperity, you are going to encounter insincere people that will try to attach themselves to you because they want something. I think it's fair to say that the best moments of your life are when you go through hardships because not only adversity will make you into a better person, but your hardships in life will reveal who's on your side. You're only going to have a few people that will endure the hardships of life with you. No matter what you do in this world, or how great of a person you are, you'll still encounter people with hidden agendas.

In knowing who you are, you must make yourself happy. As long as you're not harming anyone or breaking any laws, you may put yourself first because most of the people you run into will attempt to inject themselves into your life because they want to sabotage you. When you're an astute and upstanding individual, your enemies will try to see if they can get you to conform to their ideas. In order for the black man to succeed in this world, he has to be self-driven from the inside. You, as a black man, should motivate yourself from within and not seek validation from others. Most people that seek validation from other people will self-destruct. Keep your integrity intact by staying true to yourself.

If you live your life trying to please other people, then you will never witness the true nature of your power. Black men, if you want to know who you are, I suggest you get into the habit of spending time by yourself. It's very important that you learn how to embrace solitude because if you don't, you can never truly be self-motivated. As a result of you not being self-motivated, you are more prone to getting manipulated by society. Speaking of society, don't let anyone shame you into wanting to spend time by yourself. If people want to gain insight into how you think and what motivates you, make them earn your trust, because in life, you should never give irrelevant people access to your mind. Black men, it's okay to make others understand that they must be in good standing with you over an extended period, especially if they want to get to know you more.

Who Are You? _____

_____

What Makes You Unique?_____

_____

_____

_____

_____

What is Your Purpose in life? What are Your Goals & Aspirations? _____

_____

_____

_____

_____

_____

_____

_____

_____

_____

_____

Take A Break From Life

It's okay to take a break from life sometimes. Mostly, you'll encounter other people in your lifetime that will not have your best interest at heart. If this applies to you, don't wait to get rid of those poisonous people, especially if your goal-oriented. The reason it's imperative for you guys to take a break from life is because taking some time off gives you an opportunity to reflect on the things that can help you become a better person.

When it comes to looking out for yourself, avoid the people in your life that are trying to be a distraction. Unfortunately, you'll have people who will come into your life as a double agent. One moment, they act like they're your closest ally, and the next, they're slandering you to others to make you look bad. Avoid these types of people because all they're doing is creating instability in your life.

Once again, if you need to take a break from life, do so. There is nothing wrong with taking a break from people, especially if they're not bringing anything valuable or positive into your life. Always remember that you have to be the architect of your life and the gatekeeper of your happiness. It's your job to remove yourself from them because if you don't, they'll continue to bring more negativity into your life. Not only do you have to remove yourself from other people, you may also have to remove your inner self sometimes because maybe it's you that's the negative person and not them. Sometimes in life you have to get rid of the old you in order to become a better version of yourself. Until you look at yourself in the mirror and start holding yourself accountable, you'll never improve as a man.

Listen To Your Instincts

If your instincts are telling you something, it's likely true. Always pay close attention to everything that is transpiring in your life. Many black men end up in prison, having toxic relationships, or even dead because they were careless.

Always listen to your conscience and never ignore that inner voice in your head that's telling you to avoid dangerous situations. When you follow your instincts and you adhere to the scriptures in the bible, your life will be more fulfilling and more promising because you'll be avoiding negative energy.

Once again guys, listen to your intuition, remain thoughtful in your decision makings and always pay attention to your surroundings. This society you live in is very dysfunctional and I encourage you guys to get more involved in the scriptures and develop a more peaceful mind because that's what's going to provide stability for your life. In life, you can never go wrong with acquiring knowledge and wisdom, especially during tough times. In order to figure out a solution to your problems, address the root of your issues. No matter how you slice it, the root of your issues is going to be based on how you think, how you act, and how you respond to certain situations. Keep in mind that none of us are perfect because there will be moments in life when you'll lose your cool. Make sure you gather your thoughts and pull yourself together. Seek people who are sincere and can help you stay away from dangerous situations. The last thing

you want is to get involved in something that will lead to your demise.

Is It Worth It?

As a black man, you must understand what's beneath you. It's important that you realize certain things and certain people are just not on your level. Not all, but many of you black men are always engaging in a verbal or physical altercation with someone over something pointless and avoidable. Have you ever thought about walking away? Have you ever considered letting the situation go? I know it's hard, but you have to be smarter.

Listen, we all go through that stage in life when puberty hits. We develop some facial hair, and we want to act tough by flexing and staring at other people we don't even know. Understand that if you're not careful, an altercation can lead to you getting assaulted, going to jail, or even getting killed. As you get older and more mature, you have to identify the toxic people. Toxic people have no discipline and no motivation to better themselves. Therefore, toxic people become more concerned with creating chaos than empowering themselves.

Gentlemen, when you see a toxic or chaotic person, do everything in your power to avoid them. I promise you, it's not worth going back and forth with losers. Remember, all of you guys are gifted and talented in your own way; please don't waste your time going back and forth with a worthless person. If you know you have a purpose in life, you must do everything you can to protect yourself.

Most of these worthless people you run into come from a toxic environment and a rough upbringing. As a result, these worthless people are always looking for a reason to express their anger. It's important that you guys remain vigilant at all times because a negative person loves taking their frustrations out on people that appear more functional than them. Certain scenarios require self-defense, while other scenarios are avoidable and unnecessary.

During your lifetime, you will encounter many people that will be envious of you. Never become susceptible to these types of people because this happens all the time. Many people are envious of others because they don't invest enough quality time into their own lives. If a person is trying to create a problem in your life, it's going to be up to you to decide if you want to engage with that person. You never know who you will encounter in life, so it is important to stay focused on your own objectives.

This may sound harsh, but when you don't know the person you're dealing with, always assume that the person is crazy &/or unstable. Why? Well, it's because sometimes in life, you must expect the worst out of people. You should never underestimate the harm someone can do to you. To ensure your safety and future, make wise decisions.

Have you ever had an encounter with a toxic person? If so, what was the experience like? Did you walk away? Did you get into an altercation with them? If so, what were some things that led up to the altercation? What did you learn from your experience?

_____

_____

_____

_____

_____

_____

_____

_____

_____

_____

_____

_____

_____

_____

_____

_____

_____

Masculinity & Manhood

It's very important that you embrace your manhood and your masculinity. Understand that when society declares war on all men, their primary target is going to be the black man. As a black man, you must be mindful of the corporations you support, the "advocates" you see in the media, the celebrities you celebrate and the people you associate with because most of them, if not all of them, are seeking to sabotage you.

As it pertains to masculinity and manhood, the first person you must evaluate is yourself. Why is that? It's because, as a man, you must look at yourself in the mirror and acknowledge the things you need to improve in your life. Besides that, never allow others to dictate your way of thinking and how to live your life

Never let society shame you for being something that you naturally are. Understand that leadership, power, influence, and authority are major attributes black men should pursue, as long as their motives are pure. If you're not doing your due diligence and refusing to step up to the mantle of manhood, you're partaking in self-emasculation. Therefore, you're destroying yourself and disrupting the natural order.

A major concept that society will try to push on men in order to emasculate them is this idea of being vulnerable and sensitive. Don't buy into the misconception that most women love guys that are emotionally vulnerable. If you start to feel and express emotions like the woman does, you can't be surprised if she no longer respects you. I'm not saying men should be like robots but understand that you as the man should learn how to regulate your feelings and emotions. You don't have the luxury to have emotional breakdowns like women do. Be very careful on how you express your emotions, especially in front of a woman, because certain women are always looking for some kind of weakness in a man so she can one day exploit him.

What are your thoughts on masculinity and manhood? Do you feel like someone or something is trying to take away your masculinity and manhood?

_____

_____

_____

_____

_____

_____

_____

_____

_____

_____

_____

_____

_____

_____

_____

Don't Be Someone That You're Not

Not only you should know who you are, be who you are and don't be something or someone that you're not. Being someone that you're not is a clear indicator you're not satisfied with your life. Brothers, understand that in life, you must be satisfied with who you are. There is nothing wrong with knowing and loving yourself because being infatuated with someone else is not only weird, you're also humiliating and insulting yourself.

I'm not saying you shouldn't admire the other person's gifts and talents, but when you become envious or are a fan of that person, you'll lose your true identity. Instead of trying to investigate the things that make other people so special, you need to seek your own abilities and figure out what makes you unique. As a man, it's not wise to fulfill another person's energy and personality as opposed to just being who you are.

Who knows, as you continue to look deep within yourself, you may discover some hidden talents about yourself that you never knew you had. Whatever your gift is, I encourage you to display it to the world in a way that makes you authentic. If you are going to be like someone, strive to be like God. From a biblical standpoint, you shouldn't be obsessed with worldly things on this earth anyway, because if things were to go wrong, you wouldn't know how to handle it in a spiritual sense. Therefore, I implore you black men to spend more time by yourself because a major component of finding true happiness is being who you are.

Always remember to never live your life comparatively, because when you compare your life to others; your happiness will get taken away from you. When you look at another man's woman, house, money, car, clothes and compare it to yours, you'll become an envious person. Stop seeking what other people have and focus on yourself. When you become fixated on another person, you are no longer living your life to improve yourself.

Be Careful Around Women

It's important for black men to understand that some women are not wife material. Please understand that you cannot turn a low-quality woman into a wife, no matter how hard you try. I hope and pray that all of you guys one day find yourself a high-quality woman that will not only provide you with help and support, but she'll also bring a level of peacefulness into your life instead of destruction. However, before you bring a woman into your life, it will be best for you to get your life in order first. Make sure you are healthy and stable in every aspect of your life.

When interacting with the women you care about, be sure to love and nurture them in the best way possible. Although women are beautiful and irreplaceable, they can be capricious and unpredictable. One day, the woman will love you, and the next day she wants to kill you. Because of her nature, you as a man must monitor and pay attention to her behavior, her mannerism, and the things she says. Don't bring a woman into your life just to make things harder for her. That is unacceptable and irresponsible.

Why should the black man evaluate his life every day from moment to moment? It's because people change, including women. Black men, don't get cocky and assume that the women you deal with will never change up on you.

Understand that if it can happen to your fellow brother, it can happen to you. None of us are perfect and we will make mistakes, but understand you have to put your mind and spirit into much higher things that don't include the woman. Don't idolize and worship women because it's unhealthy and it will lead you to a destructive life. Now keep in mind if you're in a healthy relationship, you will have responsibilities to the woman, and it's important that you don't bring any negativity or instability into her life, especially if she's a wonderful woman. Even if you're happy with the woman you're with, humble yourself by understanding that she could turn on you. Remember that she is capable of betraying you, so keep this possibility in mind. That way, you won't be devastated if it happens. The primary focus for you as a black man is to remain honest and consistent because, believe it or not, men change up on women as well.

What has your experience been like so far when dealing with women? Has it been positive, negative, or both? What are your thoughts on the woman? What do you think your role is as a man when you're dealing with women?

_____

_____

_____

_____

_____

_____

_____

_____

_____

_____

_____

_____

_____

_____

_____

_____

_____

Seeking Happiness

What exactly is happiness? What does it entail? How do you get it? I want the black man to understand his own capacity for joy because not only is having it significant for him, but it is even more important to recognize where his source of fulfillment and satisfaction should come from. The first thing you need to understand as a black man is that happiness is just an emotion, not a state of being. Therefore, your focus as a black man should be about reaching satisfaction and fulfillment in your life. Many of you guys may not agree with me, but becoming a servant of God can be one way to reach contentment and fulfillment in this society.

Not to digress, but please understand that when I mention God, I am strictly referring to the bible and the scriptures, not mainstream religion. The reason I bring this up is that I don't want you brothers to conflate the two. Believe it or not, there is a difference between mainstream religion and the actual scriptures from the bible. From a biblical standpoint, the scriptures will actually inform you of what happiness is and how to seek it. If you don't believe me, check out **proverbs 16:20, proverbs 3:13 and psalms1 1:3 (just to name a few).** Unfortunately, many brothers have been led to believe that the concept of God is insubstantial, when in reality, each black man should be a physical embodiment of the heavenly angels. Yet, for a black man to be this, he must be in his correct mindset. As the sons of God, it is our responsibility to carry out our duties the best way we can. As I mentioned before, none of us are perfect and we are going to make mistakes because we are human beings.

Just because you're a black man doesn't mean you have to look at these other demographics for inspiration. Please understand that every black man has the potential to be a prominent leader, but it starts with leading yourself, your community, and presiding over your household appropriately. Having a spiritual connection with God and establishing harmony, stability and serenity in your life will bring you true contentment.

Notes

END